Our World

Flowers and Seeds

By Margaret Grieveson

Aladdin/Watts
London • Sydney

PAPERBACK EDITION PRINTED 2007

© Aladdin Books Ltd 2004

Designed and produced by
Aladdin Books Ltd
2/3 Fitzroy Mews
London W1T 6DF

First published in 2004 by
Franklin Watts
338 Euston Road
London NW1 3BH

Franklin Watts Australia
Level 17/207 Kent Street
Sydney NSW 2000

Franklin Watts is a division of
Hachette Children's Books

ISBN 978 0 7496 7770 1

A catalogue record for this
book is available from the
British Library.

Dewey Classification:
582.13

Editor:
Harriet Brown

Design:
Flick, Book Design and Graphics

Picture researchers:
Brian Hunter Smart
Harriet Brown

Educational Consultant:
Jackie Holderness – former Senior Lecturer
in Primary Education, Westminster Institute,
Oxford Brookes University

Printed in Malaysia

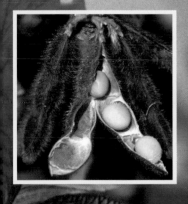

CONTENTS

Notes to parents and teachers

This series has been developed for group use in the classroom as well as for children reading on their own. In particular, its differentiated text allows children of mixed abilities to enjoy reading about the same topic. The larger size text (A, below) offers apprentice readers a simplified text. This simplified text is used in the introduction to each chapter and in the picture captions. This font is part of the © Sassoon family of fonts recommended by the National Literacy Early Years Strategy document for maximum legibility. The smaller size text (B, below) offers a more challenging read for older or more able readers.

Flowers need birds

Some flowers need birds to help them make seeds. Birds go to brightly coloured flowers in search of nectar.

A

◀ **Colourful flowers attract birds.**

Birds have a poor sense of smell so these flowers don't need to produce much scent.

B

Questions, key words and glossary

Each spread ends with a question which parents and teachers can use to discuss and develop further ideas and concepts. Further questions are provided in a quiz on page 30. A reduced version of pages 30 and 31 is shown below. The illustrated 'Key words' section is provided as a revision tool, particularly for apprentice readers, in order to help with spelling, writing and guided reading as part of the literacy hour. The glossary is for more able or older readers. In addition to the glossary's role as a reference aid, it is also designed to reinforce new vocabulary and provide a tool for further discussion and revision. When glossary terms first appear in the texts, they are highlighted in bold.

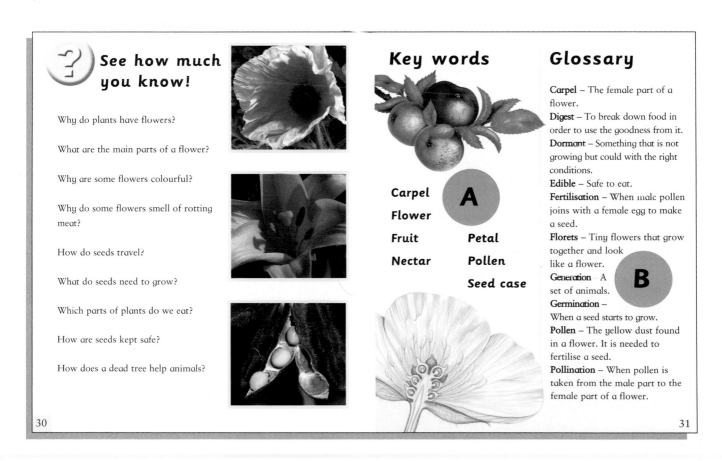

See how much you know!

Why do plants have flowers?

What are the main parts of a flower?

Why are some flowers colourful?

Why do some flowers smell of rotting meat?

How do seeds travel?

What do seeds need to grow?

Which parts of plants do we eat?

How are seeds kept safe?

How does a dead tree help animals?

Key words

Carpel
Flower

A

Fruit   Petal

Nectar   Pollen

Seed case

Glossary

Carpel – The female part of a flower.
Digest – To break down food in order to use the goodness from it.
Dormant – Something that is not growing but could with the right conditions.
Edible – Safe to eat.
Fertilisation – When male pollen joins with a female egg to make a seed.
Florets – Tiny flowers that grow together and look like a flower.
Generation – A set of animals.

B

Germination – When a seed starts to grow.
Pollen – The yellow dust found in a flower. It is needed to fertilise a seed.
Pollination – When pollen is taken from the male part to the female part of a flower.

Flowers are everywhere

Flowers are many shapes, sizes and colours. Some are big and colourful. Others are tiny. Some flowers look like leaves. Even trees and grasses have flowers. Most plants have flowers so they can make seeds. Seeds can grow into new plants.

▶ **This big pink rose is easy to see.**

The goal of every plant is to make the next **generation** of plants. Most plants do this by producing seeds. Flowers contain all the parts that a plant needs to make seeds. Insects and animals help too. This flower's bright colour and strong sweet scent make it easy for them to spot.

◀ This is the world's biggest flower.

The Rafflesia flower is the world's biggest flower. It is found in the jungles of Malaysia and can grow up to one metre wide. Instead of growing in the ground, it attaches itself to other plants. It smells of rotting meat!

One sunflower is made of lots of tiny flowers.

Flowers come in all shapes and sizes. Tulips have one bell-shaped flower at the top of the stem. Foxgloves have lots of flowers all the way up the stem. A sunflower looks like one big flower. If you look closely you will see that it is made up of lots of tiny flowers, called **florets**.

Florets

 Sunflowers are yellow. Can you name other yellow flowers?

The parts of a flower

Flowers open out from buds in spring or summer when it is warm and light. Sepals on the buds keep them warm and dry until it is time to open. Sepals are usually green and look like small leaves.

Petals

Sepals

◀ **The petals are orange and the sepals are green.**

Most flowers are made of four parts – sepals, petals, **carpels** and **stamens**. The sepals protect the flower bud. After the bud has opened, the sepals have done their job and may fall off. Petals are often brightly coloured. They surround and protect the carpel and stamens inside them. There is sugary nectar in the base of most flowers.

▲ You can see the yellow pollen on the stamens.

A seed may grow inside the carpel.

Below is a cross-section of a flower and its stem. It shows the parts of the flower. A group of carpels is called a pistil. Seeds may eventually form from the egg inside each carpel. Not all flowers have both the male and female parts.

The stamens are the male part of the flower. Stamens produce **pollen**. The carpel is the female part of the flower. In this photo, the carpel is in the middle of the stamens. Some flowers have only one carpel, but others have many.

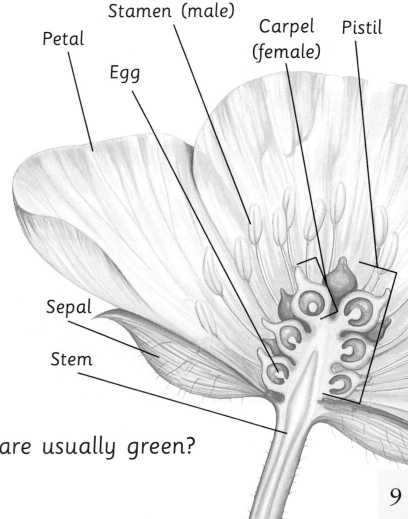

Petal

Egg

Stamen (male)

Carpel (female)

Pistil

Sepal

Stem

 Which parts of a flower are usually green?

Making seeds

To make a seed, pollen has to go from the male part of one flower to the female part of another flower. Many flowers have help from insects to move the pollen. Some plants use the wind, birds and other animals to carry pollen.

► **If a bee goes into this flower, pollen may rub off onto its legs.**

When an insect enters a flower, it rubs against the male stamens as it tries to find nectar to feed on. Sticky pollen attaches itself to the insect's back and legs. The insect then flies to another flower. Some insects are furry to make sure that even more pollen sticks to them.

The bee carries the pollen to the next flower.

Pollination is when a pollen grain lands on the carpel of a flower. Plants that use the wind to transfer pollen must produce thousands of pollen grains. This way, at least some of them reach a carpel.

Pollen joins with an egg to make a seed.

When a pollen grain lands on the sticky carpel, it grows a tube down towards the female egg. When they join they begin to produce a seed and the seed's casing. This process is called **fertilisation**.

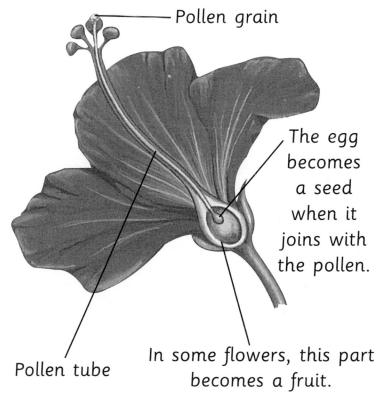

Pollen grain

The egg becomes a seed when it joins with the pollen.

Pollen tube

In some flowers, this part becomes a fruit.

 What insects have you seen visiting a flower?

11

Colour and scent

Some flowers have brightly coloured petals. When bees and other insects see these bright colours they go to the flower to search for nectar. Other flowers have strong scents so that insects will go to them.

▶ **This bee saw the petals and is looking for nectar.**

Insects see differently from humans. Some colours that look dull to us can attract insects to flowers when they are searching for nectar. Some rare flowers are very brightly coloured and have unusual shapes to attract insects who might otherwise ignore them.

◀ Some flowers have strong scents to bring insects to them.

The Buddleia bush smells so sweet and attracts so many butterflies that it is called the 'butterfly bush'. It is the nectar in the flower that smells sweet. Some flowers, such as the Rafflesia (see page 7), smell of rotting meat, which attracts flies to them.

An evening primrose looks different to a bee (below right) than it does to us.

Bees can see **ultra-violet light** so they can see flower markings that are invisible to us. The flower markings point towards the nectar, stamens and carpels in the middle of the flower. Some flowers, such as this evening primrose, even advertise a landing platform for bees (below right). This way, plants make sure that plenty of insects visit them.

 How and why do flowers attract insects?

Flowers need birds

Some flowers need birds to help them make seeds. Just like insects, some birds go to brightly coloured flowers in search of nectar. The pollen rubs off onto their beaks and feathers. They carry the pollen to other flowers.

▶ **Colourful flowers attract birds.**

Birds are heavier than insects and a bird's beak is hard. Because of this, bird-pollinated flowers are firm and tough. Birds have a poor sense of smell so these flowers don't need to have a strong scent. Unlike bees, birds are not sensitive to ultra-violet light so flowers must be brightly coloured to attract them.

◄ Humming-birds drink nectar from some flowers.

Some flowers need humming-birds to carry pollen to help them make seeds. Humming-birds also need flowers. They need the sugary nectar in these flowers for energy so that they can beat their wings up to 80 times a second!

Some bats and small animals like to drink nectar.

This tiny honey possum has a long snout and tongue for lapping up nectar from eucalyptus flowers. Its tongue can extend two centimetres from its body even though honey possums are only half the size of a mouse. Pollen rubs off onto the possum's snout and is carried from one flower to another in this way.

 Why do birds and animals visit flowers when they are hungry?

Flowering trees

Some trees have two kinds of flowers on them – male flowers and female flowers. These catkins (left) are male flowers. They are covered with pollen. The same tree also has small female flowers.

► **A holly tree can be male or female.**

Holly trees or bushes are either all male or all female. Both male and female holly trees have white flowers. Berries only form on the female trees. To make new plants, there must be a male and female holly tree growing near each other. Insects carry pollen from the male to the female tree.

◀ Both male and female flowers grow on a pine tree.

The male flowers are usually red or purple and the female flowers are often yellow or white. The female flower will become a pine cone if it is fertilised (see page 11).

Most trees and bushes have flowers.

Some trees have flowers to attract insects, while others use the wind to spread pollen. Trees that use the wind usually have green, feathery flowers that hang from the tree.

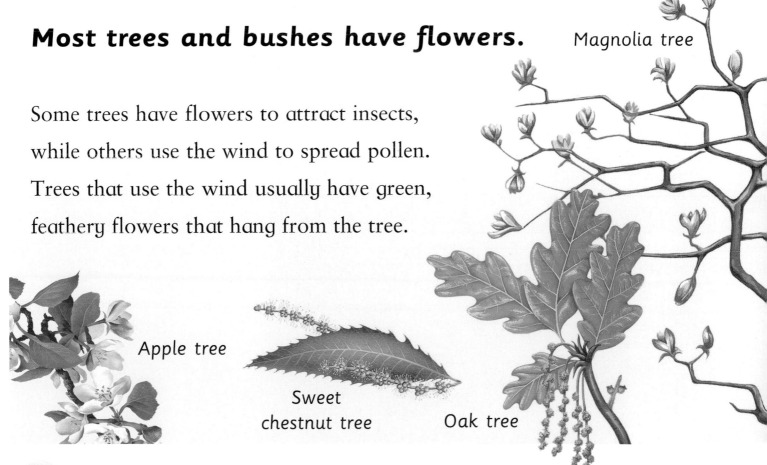

Magnolia tree

Apple tree

Sweet chestnut tree

Oak tree

 Why can catkins use the wind to carry their pollen?

Seeds

Some seeds are so tiny they look just like specks of dust. Others are as big as footballs! Most seeds do not start to grow as soon as they are made. They need to be kept safe inside a fruit or seed case until it is the right time to grow into a new plant.

Cherry

Pistachio nuts

Black-eyed peas

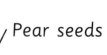

Pear seeds

▲ **Soya bean seeds**

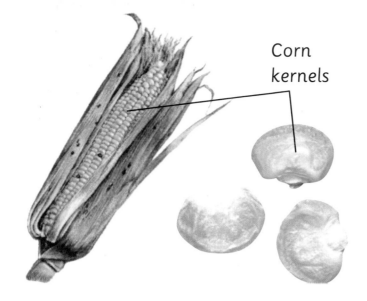

Corn kernels

▲ Orange seeds

◀▲ Most seeds grow inside a seed case or fruit.

The casing that protects a seed can be hard like a nut shell, or soft like an apple or tomato. Each seed case is adapted to help keep the seed safe.

Strawberry covered in seeds

Beans and nuts are seeds.

Inside each seed is a baby plant. This tiny plant already has a root and shoot and the food it needs to begin to grow.

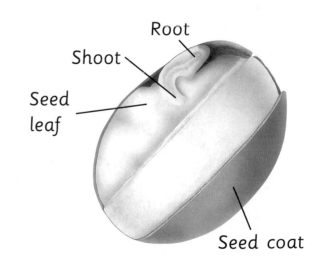

Root

Shoot

Seed leaf

Seed coat

 Which fruits and vegetables make seeds that we eat?

How seeds travel

Most new plants will grow better if they do not have to share water, soil and sunlight with a bigger plant. When seeds are made, the plant tries to spread its seeds as far away as it can. Animals, the wind and water are used to move seeds to new places.

◀ **Some seeds are blown by the wind.**

Dandelion seeds are very light and are carried by the wind. They float on the wind instead of falling straight down.

Coconuts are carried ▶ away by the sea.

Coconuts have a padded waterproof case so they can travel long distances by sea.

◀ Squirrels eat seeds.

Many fruits are tasty but the seeds have hard cases and cannot be digested. If an animal eats a seed it will come out of the other end without being harmed. It can then grow into a new plant away from the parent plant. This squirrel carries seeds in its tummy. Other animals carry seeds on their outsides. These seed cases have hooks or burrs to catch on to an animal's coat.

▼ These seeds have stuck to an animal's fur.

 Why do plants spread their seeds?

When seeds begin to grow

A seed needs water and warmth so it can start to grow into a seedling. Then it needs sunlight, soil and more water so it can grow into a full size plant. If it has too much water it will rot. If it has too little water it will dry out.

This is a bean seed. It grows a root and a shoot.

A seed can look dead, but it is often just **dormant**. Some seeds can lie dormant for hundreds of years. The time when a seed begins to grow is called **germination**. The root grows first and then the shoot appears.

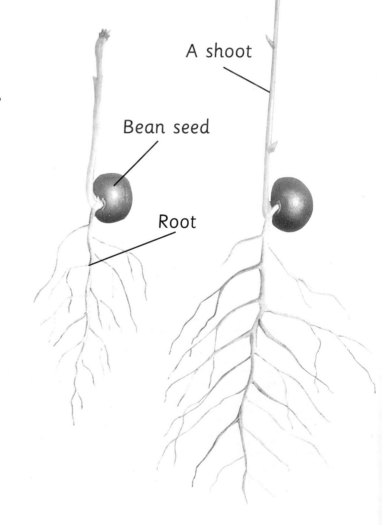

A shoot

Bean seed

Root

Beans can grow in a jar.

Soak some beans in water overnight (as shown in picture A). The next day, place the bean seeds between blotting paper and the side of a glass jar (picture B). Pour in a few centimetres of water. Put the jar on a warm, sunny window-sill. Add a little water each day. Your bean will grow a root and a shoot (picture C). When it grows too big for the jar, plant it in soil. If it has flowers and they are fertilised it will make new bean seeds.

C

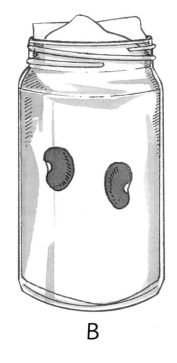

B

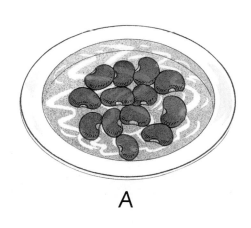

A

 Will a seedling grow well in the dark?

Life cycles

When a seed bursts into life and a new plant begins to grow, it is part of a greater life cycle. The new plant grows and makes new seeds which may grow into new plants. Dead plants also give life to other plants and animals.

A pine cone seed

1 Pine cones contain lots of seeds. They contain the information they need to make a new plant.

2 If the seed lands on soil and has water and light, it may germinate.

2

A sapling

A seedling

3 With enough light and water, the tiny plant continues to grow.

4 Once the tree is fully grown, it can make its own pine cones. When they fall, the life cycle begins all over again (1).

3

A minibeast

5 Minibeasts feed off dead plants and live inside fallen trees. Dead plants break down and their goodness returns to the soil.

6 The goodness in the soil helps other plants to grow. The space cleared by the fallen tree allows more light to reach the ground. New plants, such as ferns, may then grow.

A pine tree

Ferns

What is a young tree called?

Plants as food

People and animals need plants for food. We can eat all the different parts of plants. We can eat the stem and leaves of some plants, but sometimes we eat the roots, the fruits or the seeds.

Capers

◀ ▲ **We eat some flowers but not others.**

Did you know that broccoli (left) and cauliflowers are **edible** flowers? Capers (above) are edible flower buds. Other flowers are not at all good to eat. It is dangerous to eat some flowers. Eating this iris (lower left) would make you ill.

26

Farmers sow seeds. The seeds grow into plants for us to eat.

Farmers water their crops if there is too little rain. They harvest the crops when they are ready. If there is too much rain or wind, or it is too hot or too cold, the crops may be ruined.

We eat stems, leaves, bulbs, roots, fruits and seeds.

Look at these pictures. Some of these fruits and vegetables will be cooked, others are eaten raw. You eat the stem of a celery plant, the bulb of an onion plant and the seeds in a tomato. Wheat seeds are ground to make flour.

Apples

Onion

Tomato

Wheat

Celery

 Can you name five plants that you like to eat?

Flesh-eating plants

Some plants trap insects and suck the goodness out of their bodies. Insects go to sundews or flytraps to look for food. When they do, they may be held by sticky hairs or trapped by strong leaves that snap shut like jaws!

◀ **This plant feeds on tasty insects.**

This plant (left) catches insects on its sticky leaves. Other plants catch insects by looking and smelling good. Pitcher plants (top left) do this. The insect goes to the pitcher plant to feed on the nectar. Once inside the plant's hollow leaf, it cannot climb out because the walls are slippery. It dies in the liquid at the bottom, dissolves and becomes plant food.

▶ Insects stick to the hairs on sundew plants.

This sundew plant oozes sticky juice onto the insect. The insect isn't strong enough to escape. Its body turns to liquid and the plant absorbs the insect through its leaves!

This Venus flytrap has a fly in its jaws.

This fly has been tricked into stepping onto the leaf of a Venus flytrap while it was searching for nectar. The leafy jaws snap shut when anything touches the hairs. The Venus flytrap kills its victims using a liquid that turns the fly's body into juice. It can take the flytrap two weeks to **digest** one fly.

 How do some plants trap insects?

 **See how much you know!**

Why do plants have flowers?

What are the main parts of a flower?

Why are some flowers colourful?

Why do some flowers smell of rotting meat?

How do seeds travel?

What do seeds need to grow?

Which parts of plants do we eat?

How are seeds kept safe?

How does a dead tree help animals?

Key words

Carpel **Petal**

Flower **Pollen**

Fruit **Seed case**

Nectar **Sepal**

Stamen

Glossary

Carpel – The female part of a flower.

Digest – To break down food in order to use the goodness from it.

Dormant – Something that is not growing but could with the right conditions.

Edible – Safe to eat.

Fertilisation – When male pollen joins with a female egg to make a seed.

Florets – Tiny flowers that grow together and look like one large flower.

Generation – A new set of plants or animals.

Germination – When a seed starts to grow.

Pollen – The yellow dust found in a flower. It is needed to fertilise a seed.

Pollination – When pollen is taken from the male part to the female part of a flower.

Stamen – The male part of a flower where pollen is made and stored.

Ultra-violet light – Light that is invisible to humans.

Index